Run for the Oval Room

THE MILWAUKEE JOURNAL

November 19, 1973

'Hocus pocus . . .'

June 28, 1973

THE MILWAUKEE JOURNAL
Publishers-Hall Syndicate, 1973

RUN
FOR THE
OVAL ROOM

...they can't corner us there

BY BILL SANDERS

Preface
by George E. Reedy
Former Presidential Press Secretary

Now Dean of the College of Journalism
Marquette University

ALPHA PRESS
Milwaukee, Wisconsin

July 3, 1973

THE MILWAUKEE JOURNAL
Publishers-Hall Syndicate. 1973

'Yeah. I had a great Independence Day
celebration. How about you?'

For Joyce, Cathy, Vicky,
Cheryl and Denese

Alpha Press
10721 West Capitol Drive, Suite 201
Milwaukee, Wisconsin 53222

CONTENTS

July 26, 1973

THE MILWAUKEE JOURNAL
Publishers-Hall Syndicate, 1973

'Imagine! Congress trying to curb my right to conduct unconstitutional wars! Why, that's unconstitutional!'

PREFACE

by George E. Reedy

**Former Presidential Press Secretary
Now Dean of the College of Journalism
Marquette University**

I do not envy Bill Sanders. He practices cartooning at a moment in history when all of the dominant forces in our society appear to be in a conspiracy to make the art impossible. The fact that he performs superbly excites my admiration. But when I calculate the odds against him, I whisper a silent prayer of thanks to the Almighty that I have not been assigned the task of reducing the events of the day to a few, swift strokes of the pen. Rather Bill than me.

The art of cartooning is fundamentally one of legitimate exaggeration. The caricaturist must penetrate to the heart of an event; strip away all of the secondary details; magnify the essence and place it on a sheet of paper where it can evoke instant and virtually universal recognition. Under the best of circumstances this is a perplexing problem and the dividing line between legitimate exaggeration and invalid distortion is thin. It takes at least a slight touch of genius to stay on the right side of the line.

But, as has been noted, we are not living in times that provide the best of circumstances. How in the devil can anyone exaggerate the events of our era? What scene can express graphically the tawdriness of a vice president of the United States forced to resign and facing disbarment charges because he was on the take? What picture can capture the sadism of a White House assistant giggling over the thought of a man twisting "slowly — slowly — in the wind"?

What can pen and ink do to drive home more forcefully the insanity of the slaughter in Southeast Asia?

Our society is its own caricature — so exaggerated already that most observers are driven to sputtering impotence or numb acquiescence.

There are times when Bill Sanders comes close to sputtering but he is never impotent and he never accepts evil or inanity without protest. By some extraordinary feat of internal discipline, he has mastered the process of controlling his rage so it can be channeled into the area of maximum impact. He understands the value of passion in human discourse and understands equally well the vital necessity of using it so it will not be wasted.

What really makes Sanders an outstanding cartoonist, however, is that he has captured the essential horror of the past few decades — the modern alliance between evil and inanity. There is nothing new, except for technology, in brutality, corruption, falsehood and betrayal. These qualities have been basic elements (I hasten to add not the only elements — men and women can be noble as well as base) of the human drama since the fall from grace. But in the past the practitioners were either open as to their goals or hid behind lofty motives. The Huns and the Vikings ravaged Europe because they wanted plunder and the *conquistadores* flogged and burned helpless Indians for the greater glory of God. Such motivations did not ease the suffering of the victims but at least they were not fatuous.

This is an age in which we cover monstrous wrong with dull-witted fatuity. We have been blanketed with puerile non-explanations for so many decades that it often takes a major jolt for us to see the hideous reality. I have before me a Bill Sanders cartoon that provides such a jolt. The central character is a Supreme Court justice (personifying all the Supreme Court justices who ruled that the court could not intervene in Southeast Asia) lecturing a group of cadavers in a shell hole in Vietnam on "the complexity and importance of issues involved in restraining U.S. bombing of your country." Could anything be more eloquent in expressing the ultimate indignity we have placed on top of violent death in that distressful corner of the globe?

This theme — the juxtaposition of banality and tragedy — runs all through Bill Sanders. It is inherent in the moronic cheerfulness of the government official who is willing to "gamble" on the health of citizens who have not been properly warned about dangerous drugs. It shines in the face of the American Law Institute representative who proposes the sanctification of evidence illegally gathered. And it is personified by a President who, when accused of lying, shrugs his shoulders and says,"Well, if you want to be picky. . . ."

What Bill Sanders is trying to tell us is that the fast buck artists of our society do not even consider it necessary any more to think up plausible excuses to conceal chicanery. They believe that just words will do — any words so long as they are dull, leaden and sufficiently narcoleptic. It is probably the best measure of the danger to our institutions that vice no longer deems it obligatory to make the obeisance of hypocrisy to virtue.

There is something very reassuring to me in the fact that there are men and women on the scene who raise their voices (a pen in the hands of Bill Sanders is a voice) in outrage. Human beings who protest are not in despair. They are clinging to a faith in mortal conscience and fundamental decency which, if aroused, can be an irresistible force. More power to them!

It is for this reason that I look forward each day to the Bill Sanders cartoon. In his chronicles of the dreary malefactors of our times, he pinpoints their derelictions not only with grace and insight but also with passionate protest, and in passionate protest there is hope of redemption for our society.

America, Inc.

Something I used to hear quite often (from a fellow by the name of Richard Nixon) is how free enterprise could fix things up in this country if it weren't for the bad influence of Federal Government — which may contain an element of truth since I frequently read stories about how America, Inc., keeps getting caught fixing prices and elections.

It occurs to me that in recent years the free enterprise system is less concerned about Federal Government than it lets on. Every time we look around we find the two in bed together, grinning sheepishly.

With the help of Federal Government, America, Inc., has devised a welfare scheme for the rich which must be the envy of all those "shiftless" mothers down in the inner city who are trying to keep body, soul and children together.

At this point in time, as the saying goes, I agree with President Nixon who said (before he became Chairman of the Board), "We must make welfare payments a temporary expedient, not a permanent way of life." He added that the way welfare payments are administered today, "they create a permanent caste of the dependent — a colony within a nation."

Well said! But it seems to me that America, Inc., will lose its incentive if we don't do something about *their* welfare system, too. At the very least, we ought to make these corporate freeloaders stand in line and answer highly personal and degrading questions like ordinary welfare bums instead of flitting around the Washington cocktail circuit. It would also be a good idea to have them bring in some proof of U.S. residency — like a copy of their latest $100,000 contribution to the Committee to Reelect the President.

We should also mail their handout checks directly to the stockholders since it's common knowledge that these corporate officers have a habit of blowing their money on color television sets and booze, when they are not sleeping around and having more kids.

I remember President Nixon has also spoken at some length about finding ways to "relieve" the burden of high taxes for the workingman, but I've never found any proof of that in the budget bills that show up in Congress. While the average wage earners wait around for their "relief," the above-average wage earners, like Mr. Nixon, have been relieving themselves of paying any taxes to speak of.

In 1970 and 1971 Mr. Nixon managed to pay only $1,670.84 into the public till by deducting the value of public documents, gathered at public expense, while on the public payroll at $200,000 per year. A neat trick for a man who denounces welfare bums and frets over their loopholes.

But then Mr. Nixon is in good company because more than one hundred wealthy welfare types with incomes over $200,000 didn't pay any Federal income tax in 1971. And about 200,000 of the richest families in America, Inc., escaped an estimated $7.2 billion in

'You've got a great future in the corporate world, kid!'

Federal income taxes because the Government taxes capital gains at a far lower rate than regular income.

Another free enterprise theory of America, Inc., and its Chairman of the Board, is keeping this country a fit place in which to live environmentally. But while the Chairman expounds theory, the Company is filling our lakes and streams with such romantic items as mercury, phosphates, cyanide and taconite tailings. I know they are romantic items because I keep seeing television commercials that tell me what the Company is *really* doing is cleaning up the water by dumping that stuff into it.

The other theory I keep hearing from America, Inc., and its wholly owned subsidiary, Federal-Local Government, is how fortunate I am to live in this great technological age. Which, I guess, has some merit when you consider that all we had to do to get teflon skillets was to put a man on the moon.

My personal encounter with the Company was when I bought my first brand-new car, a 1967 Chevrolet Impala which I drove all the way up to 38,000 miles before I had to install a new transmission. However, the nearer I came to the end of my car payments, the less distance it would stray from the house. By the time I made the last payment, it wouldn't venture beyond the mail box at the end of the driveway.

Meanwhile, us crippled car owners are still waiting around for America, Inc., to build a mass transportation system to get us to work. Getting my old Impala started was a lark compared to getting money out of the Highway Trust Fund for a mass transit system. The Highway Trust Fund, incidentally, is a little $5-billion-a-year nest egg of tax money zealously guarded by the Highway Lobby so we can't interrupt their plans to pave over the United States. What you have to understand is that the mission of the highway has changed. Highways were initially built to get people from city to city. Now they are constructed to get the Highway Lobby, the Billboard Lobby and the Automobile Lobby over the slums and to the bank.

Chairman Nixon's idea of mass transportation includes flying in the Supersonic Trans-

port. That way we don't just pollute the air around our cities but also around the entire globe. However, that project would not be without its rewards. In the SST we could get to Europe in four hours — or about the same time it takes to get from the ticket counter to the airplane.

The main concern in this pollution problem, as I understand it, is to strike a balance between the environment and profits. Back in 1973 when Nixon declared a victory in the war on pollution — pollution with honor, I think he called it — he said, "Now is the time to stop the hand-wringing and roll up our sleeves and get on with the job!" Or, to put it another way, "It's every man for himself," said the elephant as he jumped up and down among the chickens.

Back in Wisconsin we said "Great!" Only instead of rolling up our sleeves we had to roll up our pants legs because we were standing in sewage waiting for our cut of the $6 billion Congress had appropriated for treatment plants that had been impounded by Mr. Nixon.

Once a year in Kitty Hawk, North Carolina, there is an annual meeting of an organization dedicated to the proposition that man will never fly. Its members' speeches are usually laced with spicy comments on the folly of Orville and Wilbur Wright's idea and man's recent attempts to conquer space. It's a tongue-in-cheek group and fun is had by all.

For several decades America, Inc., has sponsored a similar organization called Politics, Profits and Oil Forever — or PPOF for short. The difference between the two is that the members of PPOF take their illusions seriously.

PPOF is dedicated to the proposition that a well-greased palm keeps the waters calm — and the profit margins high. America's national political leaders have been lining up to have a little Texas crude laid on them for as long as I can remember. And in return America, Inc., dispenses oil depletion allowances, import quotas, mineral rights and promotes nine-miles-to-the-gallon automobiles.

PPOF's secondary function over the years has been to dispel the notion of some of its critics that man does not live by oil alone and

January 12, 1969

'Gentlemen, it's up to us to save this country from the crisis
of money becoming available to the common man!'

that someday the well will run dry. Even after Mr. Nixon, Chairman of the Board, fell into a half-empty well and ran off to warn the people, he still couldn't resist quoting the PPOF manual:

"There are only seven percent of the people of the world living in the United States and we use thirty percent of all the energy. That isn't bad. That is good. That means we are the richest, strongest people in the world and that we have the highest standard of living in the world. That is why we need so much energy and *may it always be that way*."

Meanwhile, back at the PPOF fraternity house, sometimes called the U.S. Congress, a few dissidents suggested spending more money for research and development of other sources, such as solar and fusion energy. But Mr. Nixon recognized that as heretical to the PPOF creed and impounded $20 million of the money that had been appropriated for that kind of research.

Another idea of the Chairman of the Board is that America, Inc., will enfranchise the disenfranchised blacks, Indians and Spanish Americans. As he put it, "Government cannot provide dignity and pride and self-respect. That will only come when people get that ownership, a piece of the action in America."

The trouble is a lot of minority Americans would prefer to get *away* from the action of slum landlords, gyp merchants, rigid bureaucrats and unfair laws by moving to the suburbs. This sounded like a good idea to former Housing and Urban Development Secretary George Romney, who suggested attacking exclusionary "snob" zoning. However, Chairman of the White Middle Class Board, Mr. Nixon, declared that "forced integration of the suburbs" was not exactly what he had in mind and that's when Mr. Romney became a *former* secretary.

Platitudes were OK but positive action in the struggle for equal rights was something else. Mr. Nixon moved from a position of "benign neglect" to outright opposition to the legislative tools of equality. We witnessed the U.S. Attorney General's office pleading in Federal court on behalf of delaying school integration in Mississippi and on behalf of tax shelters for "private" lily-white academies that have sprung up across the South.

Mr. Nixon declared it was all *wrong* to withhold Federal funds to force compliance with court-ordered integration, but it was all *right* to withhold congressionally appropriated funds in order to slow compliance with water pollution standards.

We then witnessed the Chairman of Moral Leadership telling us that he was opposed to "bussing for purposes of achieving racial balance," which was interesting in view of the fact that the courts have never held out bussing to "achieve racial balance." But then the Chairman has never been one to be confused by the facts!

Efforts of lesser Company officials to make free enterprise more free and enterprising for *all Americans* met with the kind of response found in a speech by former Office of Economic Opportunity dismantler Howard Phillips. He described administration dissenters as "cowardly and dishonest bureaucrats who seek personal glory and comfort by indiscriminately granting public funds to the *people* and *causes* Richard Nixon defeated in 1972."

That seems to me a euphemism for saying that Mr. Nixon's election represented a defeat for the poor, the hungry and the homeless, which, given the context of the last four years, may be more accurate than Mr. Phillips realized.

January 10, 1970

THE MILWAUKEE JOURNAL
TM ® All rights reserved
Publishers-Hall Syndicate

'Something for you and something for him. What could be fairer?'

"When we talked about the virtues of free enterprise, we meant for small businesses."

14

'For a minute there, I was afraid we'd be too late!'

'It's supposed to ward off the evil spirits of communism.'

THE MILWAUKEE JOURNAL
Publishers-Hall Syndicate, 1973

'Good hunting, kid!'

'Just a little bit down and the rest of your life to pay. Why,
friend, you can't afford not to own one!'

February 7, 1969

'Can't you see I'm busy fighting inflation?'

'Sorry, kid, but we can't have an overloaded boat.'

'What a novel idea. Applying it to the poor, too.'

'On the other hand, there are some people who don't work
who should have guaranteed incomes!'

April 21, 1971

'Take care of you in a minute, madam, as soon as I
finish this demonstration.'

'We have a chance today . . . to ensure better education . . . better housing . . . a cleaner environment . . .'

December 12, 1971

THE MILWAUKEE JOURNAL
TM ® All rights reserved 1971
Publishers-Hall Syndicate

'Run along home to your poverty and ignorance. I don't
want to alter the family relationship.'

TM ® All rights reserved
Publishers-Hall Syndicate

"I already peel my own potatoes, buy cheap cuts of meat and don't eat quite so much. Any other suggestions, Mr. Butz?"

'Please, madam. I'm trying to determine which is less
expensive . . . funerals or safety standards.'

'Hang on!'

THE MILWAUKEE JOURNAL

July 28, 1971

'Do his subsidies discourage him?'

'The difference between us is plain to see,'' said Tweedledum and Tweedledee.

December 4, 1973

'This here's my new deputy who will help guard th' bank!'

'There's certainly nothing misleading about that pitch!'

October 4, 1973

THE MILWAUKEE JOURNAL
Publishers-Hall Syndicate, 1973

"Chief Justice Burger? I hear you lobbied against the consumer protection bill because it would burden the courts."

February 16, 1973

'I can report that we are well on our way to winning the war against environmental degradation'

'Atomic waste peril? Don't be silly!'

June 17, 1969

'Say! He might turn out to be a better watchdog than that old
Texas hound we used to have.'

THE MILWAUKEE JOURNAL

'Hey, Pop! It's about time you came home!'

'Don't forget to turn out the lights. There's
an energy shortage, too, y'know!'

'Got an elbow joint?'

'An ounce of prevention is worth a ton of publicity, eh, J. B.?'

'Gee whiz! What are you so upset about? I'm not putting nearly as much in your water now as I used to.'

October 20, 1972

'I tell you he can't afford that kind of treatment!'

'*The government ought to crack down on these young radicals who feel justified in destroying public property!*'

'You got to pay for the sins of your elders, boy!'

November 10, 1972

"I don't think they're interested in colored beads anymore."

'Isn't it quaint how he's managed to maintain his simple existence in the midst of this modern age of ours?'

Pay-off

June 13, 1972

'Beat it! I'll get back to you as soon as I finish
with this publicity picture!'

'*Look what I got out of the closet, fellas! Yoo hoo, fellas!*
Where'd everybody go?'

'*Let me make my position perfectly clear.*'

'I don't know what they're talking about, do you, Lightning?'

July 31, 1973

'Yew could at least let him finish his Bigotry 101 class!'

February 17, 1972

THE MILWAUKEE JOURNAL
TM ® All rights reserved
Publishers-Hall Syndicate

'Remember, kid . . . I'm in your corner!'

'Nice spacecraft you got there.'

THE MILWAUKEE JOURNAL

November 7, 1971

THE MILWAUKEE JOURNAL

TM ® All rights reserved 1971
Publishers-Hall Syndicate

57

THE MILWAUKEE JOURNAL
TM ® All rights reserved 1971
Publishers-Hall Syndicate

February 14, 1972

'Beat it, kid! There ain't nobody here but us chickens!'

POWER TO CIRCUMVENT CONGRESSIONAL OEO LEGISLATION

US DISTRICT COURT

'The Emperor doesn't really have any new clothes on!'

April 11, 1969

American Gothic

61

Big Brothers

Civil liberties have always been a dilemma to this land of the free. The dichotomy is: It sounds great in principle but slightly subversive when practiced. The Bill of Rights, for example, is given a mandatory lick and a promise in high school, then stuffed into the shelves when dealing with kids.

School administrators and boards have yet to show as much concern for the depth of student learning as the length of their hair, and books are still considered a threat in many quarters.

Consider for a moment the new rules proposed in July of 1973 by the Arizona Board of Education: "Textbooks presented for adoption shall not include language or illustrations which are blatantly offensive; would cause embarrassing situations in the classroom . . . or contribute to civil disorder, social strife or flagrant disregard of the law."

Sounds like a simple solution but it does raise a question as to how the Big Brothers would deal with "contributors" to "social strife" such as Thomas Paine, Thomas Jefferson and Martin Luther King, not to mention the Boston Tea Party. The Arizona Big Brothers would be well advised to contact their counterparts in Drake, North Dakota, to learn how to really handle the situation.

There, the local school board, acting on the complaint of a coed, met and agreed that Kurt Vonnegut's novel *Slaughterhouse Five* was a "tool of the devil" and burned the school's five copies. While they were about it, they tossed in a few others, including James Dickey's *Deliverance* and an anthology that included short stories by Ernest Hemingway, William Faulkner and John Steinbeck, all winners of Nobel Prizes for literature.

If school boards and administrations have a dim view of civil liberties and the Bill of Rights, some local public officials are downright blind on the subject.

Dane County, Wisconsin, Circuit Judge William Sachtjen issued a decision denying unemployment compensation benefits to an insurance secretary who was fired for calling her boss "stupid" at a cocktail lounge after working hours. Said Judge Sachtjen, in an example of penetrating Orwellian logic: "An employee has no license to exercise any freedom of speech after working hours when the language is critical of his superiors. To hold otherwise would result in a complete breakdown of the employee-employer relationship."

Big Brother Sachtjen obviously didn't consider his ruling a "breakdown" of several principles his forefathers thought rather important when they founded this nation.

Big Brothers have always been more plentiful than ticks on a hound dog, but nowhere are they more parasitic than when wielding

levers of judicial powers out of ignorance. A former Milwaukee County judge, Christ T. Seraphim, used to take his first name seriously and the Bill of Rights in vain frequently when he ascended to sit at the right hand of Justice.

Seraphisms abound in the files of that court but the classic example had to do with a defendant the judge allowed to plead guilty without adequately being told of the Constitutional rights he would give up as a result of his plea. When a new attorney for the man attempted to withdraw the guilty plea before Seraphim — pointing out that the defendant was not advised of certain rights as required by a U.S. Supreme Court decision in the case of Boykin vs. Alabama — Seraphim reportedly replied, "Forget about Boykin, Seraphim has now ruled."

I remember back in 1968 Richard Nixon told a national radio audience that "It's time we once again had an open administration . . . open to ideas from the people, and open in its communication with the people, . . ." which sounded like a good thing at the time. Unfortunately Candidate Nixon hadn't checked that "communications" business with Big Brother Nixon who had an entirely different idea.

In the next few years a substantial number of Americans were trying to communicate to the White House their reservations and opposition to the war in Southeast Asia but found the line was busy. One of these people was Daniel Ellsberg who had the silly notion that his fellow countrymen might benefit from some details of the historical policy decisions regarding Vietnam that were made prior to the Nixon administration. The trouble with this was that it exposed the intellectual warts that government has traditionally kept from the public view.

When the "effete" press had the audacity to publish this "classified" information, Big Brother Nixon decided that the media was taking the First Amendment too seriously. For the first time in American history, we saw a President of the United States attempt to exercise prior censorship over the nation's newspapers.

The White House argued that publication of the Pentagon Papers would do "irreparable injury" to national security. Fortunately, the U.S. Supreme Court — not yet entirely corrupted — pointed out the facts of life to the administration, saying, "There is not here a showing of an immediate threat to the national security which in close and narrowly defined circumstances would justify prior restraint on publication. The Government has failed to meet its burden and without that burden being met, the First Amendment remains supreme."

But Big Brothers, unlike old soldiers, don't fade away, they just keep trying! Being fond of "firsts," President Nixon tried for another one in the guise of a proposal to revise the Federal Criminal Code. Hidden deep in that complex piece of legislation was a little jewel called the "official secrets act." The likes of that concoction hadn't been seen since Nero's mother fed her husband a bowl of mushrooms laced with arsenic!

As proposed, it would punish newsmen who published "classified" defense or foreign policy information *regardless of whether or not it damaged national security*. Not only would it punish reporters but *all* responsible officials of the publication or broadcasting company who participated in making the unauthorized information public. Under this proposal, a reporter who uncovered Government fraud or waste or criminal activity in a document that was "classified," and published it, would be subject to a jail sentence. The result would force the press to rely on Government releases — which would suit Big Brother just fine.

Now this is not to make light of Government "classification" because it is a serious business. For example, in 1960 the Pentagon was busy "classifying" all information that indicated we were using monkeys in some of our space shots. At the same time thousands of tourists passing a certain monkey cage in the Washington National Zoo were confronted with a sign which explained that the monkey on display was a research animal that had traveled into space in an American rocket.

The sign proved to be incorrect. The monkey inside was really the author of the Government classification guidelines.

The Nixon White House is also aware that a good many Americans get their news and commentary from television and he had no

May 25, 1971

"The basic idea, your honor, is to improve law enforcement by violating the law."

intention of slighting that media. The administration drafted tough new legislation that would hold individual television stations accountable, at the risk of losing their licenses, for the content of all network material they broadcast. In the words of Mr. Clay T. Whitehead, director of the White House Office of Telecommunications Policy, "Station managers and network officials who fail to act to correct imbalance or consistent bias in the networks . . . or who acquiesce by silence . . . can only be considered willing participants, to be held fully accountable . . . at license renewal time."

This is a fancy way of saying that Big Brother Government will ultimately decide what is good for us to see and hear on our local television stations.

So much for newspapers and television. Now the only things left to put under control are books, magazines and movies.

When I was a kid I sneaked into the local movie house to see Jane Russell in "The Outlaw." I remember that I couldn't quite figure out what all the scandal was about since it was tame stuff compared to the material pilfered from parents and circulated around school.

Since then I have been mildly obsessed with seeing that which others decree should not be seen. I could hardly wait to reach that magic age that would be my passport to the forbidden fruits of expression that were then reserved for the older and affluent. Little did I know that reaching that magic age would not put me beyond the reach of those Brothers who are still dedicated to keeping me pure of heart, soul, eye, ear, mouth and brain.

When the President's Commission on Pornography released its report in 1970, one would have thought they had recommended fornicating in the streets at high noon judging by the reactions from the White House and Congress. Good old Spiro Agnew was quick to disavow the report. Said Mr. Clean: "No sir, your honor, it's not our baby. As long as Richard Nixon is President, Main Street is not going to turn into Smut Alley."

If Mr. Agnew had taken the time to read the report he would have discovered some interesting findings. For example, after substantial empirical research, the Commission concluded there was no evidence that "exposure to or use of explicit sexual materials play a significant role in the causation for social or individual harms such as crime, delinquency, sexual or non-sexual deviancy or severe emotional disturbances."

However, old mythology and religious superstition die hard. In the latest Supreme Court obscenity ruling, Chief Justice Burger decreed that "although there is not conclusive proof of a connection between antisocial behavior and obscene material," state legislatures "could quite reasonably determine that such a connection does or might exist." In other words, don't be confused by the facts!

Justice William R. Rehnquist, Milwaukee's contribution to the judicial Stone Age, was less subtle in linking crime with sexual explicidness. In a case involving a California bar that featured nude acts, Rehnquist said, "Prostitution, indecent exposure to young girls, attempted rape, rape itself and assaults on police officers took place immediately adjacent to such premises."

Using Justice Rehnquist's logic a good case could be made for closing down the Supreme Court since it is a matter of record that similar crimes have taken place within blocks of the Supreme Court building.

President Nixon, commenting on the lack of evidence linking pornography and crime, said: "If that were true, it must also be true that great books, great paintings and great plays have no ennobling effect on man's conduct. Centuries of civilization and ten minutes of common sense tell us otherwise."

I don't know about "ennobling" effect but it's obvious that Mr. Nixon's reading of great works has had little *educational* effect on him. Otherwise he would know that such works as Shakespeare, Chaucer, Cervantes, Aristophanes and Molière (to mention a few) contain quite a bit of what Mr. Nixon would label "smut." I do know President Nixon saw the movie "Patton" three times. Perhaps that explains his bombing policy in Southeast Asia.

But Big Brother would suggest that all this is just rhetorical sophistry. What is important is his contention that adult American citizens cannot be trusted to openly encounter sexual material. If we are to indulge our human and quite natural drives, it must be done behind a mask of hypocrisy. It is the American way.

It matters not that American adults have been covertly exposed to about as much pornography, proportionately, as Danish adults in wide-open Copenhagen, and that a majority (almost sixty percent) believe that adults should be allowed to read or see any explicit sexual material they want to.

What matters is that our self-appointed guardians know what is best for us. They are the authors of our morals and the selectors of our liberties. All this does raise an interesting question, however: *"Quis custodiet ipsos custodes?"* Who shall guard our guardians?

August 27, 1971

'I would have preferred a hearing myself.'

March 30, 1971

'Well, they said the new Post Office Department would be more efficient.'

68

As Different as Black and White

THE MILWAUKEE JOURNAL

'Why, what was wrong with the way I tried those no
good, low down, guilty pinkos?'

November 12, 1971

THE MILWAUKEE JOURNAL

'Frankly, I don't see anything extreme
about Mr. Rehnquist's political leanings.'

'I tried my best to keep her in the cave for you.'

June 30, 1972

'Nonsense, lad. It's just your imagination!'

Publishers-Hall Syndicate 1972

THE MILWAUKEE JOURNAL

'Goodness! We're not trying to stifle her voice! We're just trying to purify it!'

'It's nothing important. Now you just run along
and go back to sleep.'

'I really appreciate what you tried to do . . . honest . . . but it just wouldn't have looked right!'

November 16, 1971

'Hello dear. I see the president didn't like your
newscast again tonight.'

FREE PRESS

THE MILWAUKEE JOURNAL   Publishers-Hall Syndicate

'PUT IT BACK!'

June 21, 1969

'Free press? Man, we don't even believe in free speech!'

'Lights! Cameras! Programming as I want it!'

April 9, 1969

'Why, that nut was trying to water my desert!'

'We hear that you have the ridiculous idea that freedom of the press includes the right to criticize our administration.'

Loneliest Man in Washington

'Now you can go back to telling mature adults
what they cannot see or read!'

December 11, 1972

September 18, 1972

NEWS ITEM: DANE COUNTY DEPUTIES BORROW STAG FILMS FOR PRIVATE VIEWING

THE MILWAUKEE JOURNAL

'There's nothin' like cold beer and porno movies after a hard day protectin' th' community morals, right, fellas?'

'Look. I'll tell you the score after the game. What could
be fairer than that?'

September 30, 1970

'Sorry, but we can't have the people electing a president!

'Now I suppose there will be a big push to disclose more of this vital data to the general public!'

'Halt!'

'Next thing y'know they'll be tellin' us the earth is not flat!'

October 7, 1970

THE MILWAUKEE JOURNAL
TM ® All rights reserved 1970
Publishers-Hall Syndicate

'I don't know what you chicks are complaining about. We're just trying to protect your feminine mystique.'

Jack Radical, Anti-Amerikan Boy

In the latter part of the 1960's the anti-war movement was reaching a crescendo on university campuses across the nation. As with any movement the ranks of the sincere are often sprinkled with hangers-on and demagogs who sour the basic principles of the issue and cloud the perspective of those trying to evaluate it.

The result is often a blanket indictment such as the one President Nixon made when he said, "You know you see these bums, you know, blowing up campuses. Listen, the boys on the college campuses today are the luckiest people in the world . . . going to the greatest universities . . . and here they are, burning up the books, storming around about this issue. I mean . . . you name it. Get rid of the war and there'll be another one."

At the same time Al Capp was making a similar judgement through his cartoon series about SWINE, Students Wildly Indignant about Nearly Everything.

I disagreed with that kind of broadside. I was, however, becoming increasingly concerned about the direction anti-war protests were taking. It was about this time that I invited three local "movement" young people to participate in a panel discussion at my church. After the affair we adjourned to my home for a rap session.

I asked one of the young men, a local leader of Students for a Democratic Society, how he squared his lofty rhetoric about freedom and democracy with the shouting down of speakers such as Hubert Humphrey when they would appear on university campuses. His reply was, "People like Humphrey and Freeman (then Secretary of Agriculture) have had years in public office to express their views . . . and their views are no longer worth hearing."

It was then I decided that if the "movement" was being swept up with the idea that there is a statute of limitations on freedom of speech, then it was embracing the same concepts held by its opponents.

In August of 1970 the fruit of that philosophy was harvested on the campus of the University of Wisconsin. Three "movement" students exploded a bomb in the Mathematics Research Center at Sterling Hall, killing a staff member of the physics department.

Moreover, the reaction to that death by many "movement" students was that it was one of those unfortunate accidents that happen in the course of a necessary action, a reaction that might well have been authored by the White House in regard to any Vietnamese civilians who were killed on a U.S. bombing run.

It seemed to me intellectually dishonest not to express my feeling that *any means* do not justify the end! And everyone going along with such a mode of operation was contaminating the democratic process. That is when I conceived and drew the "Jack Radical, Anti-Amerikan Boy" comic strip.

JACK RADICAL — THE ANTI-AMERIKAN BOY! Sanders

MAN, I'M BUSHED! I'VE BEEN OUT FIGHTING FASCISM, RACISM AND IMPERIALISM ALL DAY!

HOW DID YOU BECOME SUCH AN OPPRESSION FIGHTER, JACK?

THE HARD WAY! I WAS BORN IN A SIMPLE STONE CABIN WITH ONLY ONE SWIMMING POOL TO STUDY BY.

IT WAS TOUGH! WHY, I HAD TO DRIVE TWO OR THREE MILES TO SCHOOL EVERY DAY!

GREENBACK HIGH SCHOOL

CONTINUED TOMORROW

JACK RADICAL — THE ANTI-AMERIKAN BOY!

ONE DAY AS I SAT BY WALDEN'S POND READING MARCUSE, IT DAWNED ON ME (ABOUT THE TIME I GOT MY DRAFT CLASSIFICATION) THAT I WAS OPPRESSED BY THE ESTABLISHMENT... THAT AMERIKAN IMPERIALISTS WERE OPPRESSING ALL US TRUE, PURE, FREEDOM LOVERS!

ELDRIDGE CLEAVER HAD BEEN OPPRESSED BY MARTIN LUTHER KING... ACID FREAKS ARE OPPRESSED BY TIMOTHY LEARY....

STUDENTS ARE BEING OPPRESSED BY THE AMERIKAN CIVIL LIBERTIES UNION

AND DR. SPOCK IS BEING OPPRESSED BY SENATOR FULBRIGHT!!

WOW! UP AGAINST THE WALL!

TOMORROW: BRILLIANT DEDUCTION

BY SANDERS

96

JACK RADICAL — THE ANTI-AMERIKAN BOY!

BY SANDERS

JACK RADICAL — THE ANTI-AMERIKAN BOY!

IT'S NOW OBVIOUS WHAT WE MUST DO. WE HAVE NO CHOICE BUT TO **BLOW UP** THE **ENGLISH DEPARTMENT!**

NOW WAIT A MINUTE, MAN! THAT'S A LITTLE DRASTIC ISN'T IT?

WHAT KIND OF CHICKEN RADICAL ARE YOU? THEY TEACH **ENGLISH** THERE...RIGHT? THE **ARMY** SPEAKS ENGLISH...RIGHT? SO THAT MAKES THE **ENGLISH** DEPARTMENT PART OF THE **MILITARY GENOCIDE** PROGRAM...RIGHT?

WELL...IF YOU PUT IT THAT WAY...

BLOOEY!

TOMORROW: STEP TWO

BY SANDERS

JACK RADICAL — THE ANTI-AMERIKAN BOY!

JACK RADICAL — THE ANTI-AMERIKAN BOY!

MORAL: HE WHO WILL JUSTIFY ANY MEANS, WILL END UP JUST A MEANS.

Ours Is Not to Reason Why

In January of 1963 I was preparing for a background trip to Washington. I decided to write Pierre Salinger, President Kennedy's press secretary, and ask to look around the working wing of the White House.

After attending the regular evening news briefing in Salinger's office, he suggested that I return later and he would arrange for me to meet with the President, which I did. While waiting in Evelyn Lincoln's office, just off the oval room, I noticed a sheaf of papers in slight disarray on the corner of her desk.

One paper particularly caught my attention because it was filled with scribbling and doodles. However, one word was somewhat isolated and readable. It said simply "Vietnam" and was underlined.

The year 1962 had been the year of the Cuban missile crisis but events in Vietnam were gradually moving to center stage. Under the influence of General Maxwell Taylor, Kennedy had begun a slow buildup of U.S. forces there. However, the regime of Ngo Dinh Diem was under constant fire from a small group of American journalists for his increasingly repressive tactics.

Kennedy dispatched John Mecklin, a former Time-Life correspondent with considerable experience in Vietnam, to reassess the situation. Mecklin's report in April of 1963 was said to have started the President on a modified course for the United States in that part of the world.

My own view of Vietnam was historically abbreviated in those early years, as it was with most Americans. Few really knew much of the French colonization of what is now Vietnam, Laos and Cambodia or how it had destroyed the rural peasant society, siphoned the region's raw materials and developed a sycophantic class of Vietnamese elitest that U.S. policy would later inherit.

Few Americans were familiar with the fact that during the post-World War I Versailles Conference, a young expatriate in France, Nguyn Ai Quoc, pleaded for independence for his people in Annam (now Vietnam) and sought American help for ending French colonial rule. We ignored his appeal and the young expatriate turned to the international communist movement for support.

Few of us were aware that when the Japanese invaded Vietnam in 1940 our friends, the French colonialists, offered no resistance on orders from its traitorous Vichy government, which was cooperating with Nazi Germany. In 1945, the Japanese installed a Vietnamese aristocrat by the name of Bao Dai as "Emperor." After the war, the French kept Bao Dai as a puppet "President" in order to use him as a conduit for U.S. aid to help buttress their colonial oppression.

Fewer still were aware that during those latter days of World War II, the U.S. was working closely with a guerrilla leader in the jungles of northern Vietnam. He was the same man whose appeal we had turned down at the Versailles Conference years earlier — only now he was known as Ho Chi Minh.

Historical perspective has never been a strong foundation of American culture and politics. We generally take a short view of it and tend to write it like a script for a John Wayne shoot-'em-up.

April 28, 1972

THE MILWAUKEE JOURNAL

'We must not falter. For all that we have risked and all
that we have gained over the years now hangs
in the balance . . .'

For example, when then Vice President Hubert Humphrey was addressing a U.S. Embassy pep rally for the staff in Saigon, he called our Vietnam policy "our great adventure." Then he added, "But it is wonderful to make it, make history in your own way and in your own time."

I'm sure Humphrey didn't realize how accurate his comments were at the time. About then a book was being circulated across the U.S. titled *Why Vietnam*. It was written by Frank N. Trager, a supporter of U.S. policy in Vietnam, and was a justification for our actions there. It was published by Praeger who gave it eloquent promotion. However, they failed to mention that the book was financed by the United States Government, at taxpayers' expense, to the tune of $8,250.

For what purpose? Why, to make history in our own way. In the words of Reed Harris, then United States Information Agency official in charge of book development: "That is a program under which we can have books written to our own specification, books that would not otherwise be put out, especially those books that have strong anti-communist content and follow themes that are particularly useful for our purposes. Under the book development program, we control the thing from the very idea to the final edited manuscript." So much for historical perspective.

I was in Vietnam in November of 1967 with several other cartoonists on a tour. We finally went to Cam Ranh Bay for a two-day rest. Willard Mullin, the famous sports cartoonist, used the occasion to pick up an inexpensive bottle of Beefeaters gin at the giant base PX. As he walked out of the building, delighted with his bargain, he said jokingly, "This ain't a war — it's a way of life!"

Indeed, it had become that with the election of Lyndon B. Johnson. It was a way of life for the armchair generals, the military-industrial complex and the super-patriots in Congress. However, for the "grunts" — those lowly Marines and GI's doing the fighting — it was a way of death. After running on a campaign promise that he would not send American boys to die in an Asian war, Johnson did precisely that.

Determined not to be humiliated by what he called a "raggedy-ass little fourth-rate power," Johnson raised the level of American involvement from 16,000 troops at the beginning of 1964 to a high of 541,500 in 1969 while claiming incredibly that he was not changing U.S. policy.

President Johnson's attempts to justify the war sometimes reached comic proportions. In 1967, the administration claimed that the enemy was creating a severe military imbalance by moving twenty-five thousand tons of arms into the south from North Vietnam. This was based on an announcement by the U.S. military claiming to have sighted 2,200 trucks making their way south.

Most of the North Vietnamese trucks were Soviet vehicles able to carry 2.5 tons, which made for some interesting mathematics. At capacity load, these trucks would be carrying approximately five thousand tons. Unfortunately, that still left twenty thousand tons to be accounted for. One could only conclude that the remaining tonnage must have been carried on the backs of Asian monkeys swinging through the trees down the Ho Chi Minh Trail.

Lyndon Johnson's "nail the coonskin to the wall" policy became frayed with the constant abrasion of dissent and a growing awareness of the cost of what we were doing in Vietnam. The electronic media brought the war into America's living room in full color. Suddenly it was shorn of the euphemisms and exposed to the bare bones of death and destruction. For what? National Security, a term so patently transparent that it was quickly changed to freedom for South Vietnam.

President Nixon came into office with a secret plan to end the war. The plan as it turned out was to substitute Vietnamese bodies for American bodies in order to save face. As Nixon put it back in 1968, "I've come to the conclusion that there's no way to win the war. But we can't say that, of course."

Of course not! For to say that was to admit that we had made a mistake in the first place.

So to save face we "incurred" Laos and Cambodia. We brought in paid mercenaries

'This part about the Tet offensive being a setback . . . that's all
wrong. It was a great victory. Then, this part about . . '

from Thailand and Korea to give the war a multilateral look. We started protective reaction bombing, a euphemism for dropping more bombs on Vietnam than we dropped during the entire course of World War II. The final face-lifting act saw Nixon unleash the most barbaric bombing since the destruction of Dresden in World War II.

Waves of B-52 bombers flew missions over the population centers of Hanoi and Haiphong, dropping twenty thousand tons of bombs. White House spokesmen, with straight faces, denied it was terror bombing and assured the nation that we were hitting only military targets. The hypocrisy of that claim was exposed when Admiral Thomas Moorer, Chairman of the Joint Chiefs of Staff, appeared before the House Armed Services Committee and testified that he was *not* consulted before the bombing order was placed into effect.

Lying has always played a part in our Government's policy in Southeast Asia, but Nixon elevated it several notches in standard procedure. In 1972, he told the American public, with a straight face, that we were respecting the "neutrality" of Cambodia. He knew as he spoke the words that he was lying. He had not only authorized the secret bombing but had also authorized the official falsification of records to cover it up.

When the covert bombing war was finally exposed in 1973, Nixon defended it, saying it would have been "ludicrous" to respect Cambodia's neutrality while North Vietnam didn't. He added that given their use of the territory, we were under "no moral obligation" to honor Cambodian neutrality. In other words, two wrongs make it right.

Moreover, the question never arose as to why, if Nixon's Vietnamization was so successful, a one-million-man South Vietnamese army could not protect twenty-five thousand withdrawing American soldiers. Or, conversely, if a one-million-man South Vietnamese army could not protect twenty-five thousand withdrawing Americans, how could they possibly protect the entire area of South Vietnam after we were gone?

There used to be a standard joke about Vietnam that we should simply declare a victory and get out. I'm sure its originator never dreamed Nixon would do just that.

In the last days of his crumbling 1972 Presidential campaign, Senator George McGovern made a policy statement on Vietnam. He said that he would end American involvement in Vietnam within ninety days of taking office and would send his Vice President, Sargent Shriver, to Hanoi to speed the return of American prisoners. This, of course, brought shrieks and howls from the White House political goon squad. Secretary of Defense Melvin Laird led the party line accusing McGovern of advocating "surrender" and sending Shriver to expedite the terms.

Then in January of 1973, Nixon appeared on national television to tell the world that he was ending American involvement in Vietnam within sixty days, thus facilitating the release of U.S. prisoners, and was sending Dr. Henry Kissinger to Hanoi to expedite the terms of the arrangement. The ultimate irony of Vietnam was revealed in Dr. Kissinger's explanation of the "peace with honor" settlement.

First, it discreetly ignored the presence of over one hundred thousand of what Nixon had previously described as "invading troops" from a "country armed with the most modern weapons by major powers."

Second, it left the legitimate authority over South Vietnam up to "political evolution" (translation: grabs) after having professed all those years to knowing *exactly who* the legitimate authority was and insisting that we were defending it from an "invading" country.

Third, Dr. Kissinger, in delineating the question of legitimacy said, "This is what the *civil war* has been all about." Civil war?

So we came full circle. Vietnam, in the end, was described by its perpetrators with the same words used by its critics from the beginning. And in the interim? Fifty thousand American youths gone — mostly our least educated (only five percent of enlisted men were college graduates). Over 1.3 million Vietnamese gone. Over $55.5 billion in taxes gone.

While in Vietnam, I visited an evacuation hospital outside Saigon. In the emergency room a doctor urged me to draw a caricature for a severely wounded soldier. Perhaps it would help distract him, even if only for a moment. He was young. They all seemed incredibly young. There was a trace of a smile as he gazed through puffed eyelids and the twilight haze of sedation at the caricature. The red stain of his life seeped through the bandages on his head, chest and legs. He had been ripped by shrapnel. Later I asked the doctor if he would live. He replied flatly, "I doubt it."

How does one distract the final moments of a doomed man? Why, the same way two Presidents sought to justify the war in Vietnam and all those men, women and children who died as a result of it — by handing out a caricature of the truth.

February 8, 1972

'Anything Secretary Rogers can do, I can do better . . .'

'This isn't working. Maybe we should wallpaper it with pictures of Jane Fonda!'

April 4, 1970

'This ought to give those Yankees something to worry about besides Vietnam.'

COST OF DROPPING 400,000 TONS OF BOMBS ON VIETNAM IN NINE MONTHS

DOMESTIC CUTS

'We have to be prudent in how we spend money these days!'

"Remember now, you're under strict orders not to hit any dikes, hospitals, schools or other civilian targets!"

'The Senate wants to keep combat troops out of Laos. Didn't they believe the president when he said we weren't here?'

'Now don't get the idea we're getting involved in Cambodia . . . we're just continuing our support of South Vietnam.'

'The theory is that what you don't know won't hurt us.'

January 22, 1971

Latest casualty in Cambodia

'As you can see, our withdrawal plan is working nicely!'

August 15, 1972

THE MILWAUKEE JOURNAL
TM ® All rights reserved
Publishers-Hall Syndicate

July 19, 1973

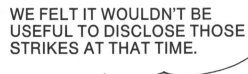

THE MILWAUKEE JOURNAL
Publishers-Hall Syndicate, 1973

THE MILWAUKEE JOURNAL

'Contrariwise,' said Tweedledee, 'if it was, it
might be; and if it were so, it would be; but as
it isn't, it ain't. That's logic.'

July 30, 1973

THE MILWAUKEE JOURNAL
Publishers-Hall Syndicate, 1973

'Are we running a Defense Department
or a hire-the-handicapped program?'

October 28, 1973

THE MILWAUKEE JOURNAL
Publishers-Hall Syndicate, 1973

March 3, 1970

'And to my left, the South Vietnamese government is demonstrating the self-determination we're fighting for.'

THE MILWAUKEE JOURNAL

'Congratulations, President Thieu! You have just won by
an overwhelming majority!'

Permanent Prisoners Of War

'They told me I was dying for national
security. As it turns out I died for national vanity.'

January 28, 1973

'Honor? What Honor?'

THE MILWAUKEE JOURNAL

Publishers-Hall Syndicate, 1973

'Of course, if you were a general who had illegally bombed North Vietnam, falsified records and retired on a fat pension, I might feel differently.'

May 24, 1973

'Gee, it must be nice to be a hero and have a
friend in the White House.'

"We want a complete reversal of the verdict."   — Milwaukee, Wis.

"Lt. Calley should receive the medal of honor."   — Rossville, Ga.

"Please save this true and great American patriot, Lt. Calley."   — West Point, Ga.

"How could you? It was clearly self-defense."   — Tampa, Fla.

"Court martial should never have taken place." — US Congressman

"I am saddened to think that one could fight for his flag and then be court martialed and convicted for apparently carrying out his orders."   — US Congressman

September 7, 1972

THE MILWAUKEE JOURNAL
TM ® All rights reserved
Publishers-Hall Syndicate

'Our final conclusion is that the blood of this tragedy is entirely on the hands of Lt. Calley.'

" . . . *for his supporting role in 'Calley, The National Hero.'* "

March 31, 1971

'It's not so difficult once you get the hang of it.'

THE MILWAUKEE JOURNAL

Watergate Warm-up

The Nixon Law and Order Team has been warming up for Watergate since the days when they were in the minor leagues. Their record has been built almost entirely on plays outside the generally accepted norms of moral and ethical play, beginning in 1946 when they took on Representative H. Jerry Voorhis. Under Coach Richard Nixon's game plan, Voorhis was not just a "new dealer," he was an enemy of the people, a subversive unfit for public office.

Operating from the right wing, his team scored again in 1952 when denouncing the Truman Administration for its alleged failure to stand up to Communist China. He described Illinois Governor Adlai Stevenson as "Adlai the appeaser . . . who got a Ph.D. from Dean Acheson's College of Cowardly Communist Containment."

And who can forget their great game against Helen Gahagan Douglas, whom they branded as disloyal to America, and whose husband, actor Melvyn Douglas, they accused of weird involvement in strange cults. The team's final play of that game came on the morning of election day when thousands of voters found on their doorstep the famous "pink sheet" intimating that Mrs. Douglas was a traitor and an agent of Communism.

One of the team members who scored on that play was Murray Chotiner, the same Murray Chotiner who was shown in a 1956 Senate investigation to have been engaged in influence peddling. Said Coach Nixon at the time, "It was a tragedy that he had to get involved in the kind of law business that does not mix with politics."

It was not the sort of "tragedy" that would warrant Mr. Chotiner's removal from a Nixon team, however. Indeed, Mr. Chotiner was on the team until he died in January 1974, practicing the same "kind of business" he had earlier, doing political hatchet work and acting as a conduit for political money from special interests.

In 1962 Nixon picked up another team player while scrambling desperately to upset incumbent Edmund G. (Pat) Brown in the California gubernatorial election. During that game one of the big plays was a bogus, 900,000 postcard "poll" that purported to show that nine out of ten rank and file registered Democrats flatly rejected the "ultra liberal" California Democratic Council that was backing Brown.

The postcard poll was mailed with a covering letter that was laced with such scare phrases as "takeover by left-wing forces whose objectives are foreign to those of most Americans," and "left wing cancer." It was a fraudulent poll, part of an operation that included generated letters and bogus front groups.

Who conceived and directed that operation? Why, the new team member, Mr. H. R. Haldeman. Who approved it? Why, Coach Richard Nixon. Who said so? California Superior Court Judge Byron Arnold, in issuing an injunction against the Team: "This postcard poll was reviewed, amended and finally approved by Mr. Nixon personally."

As the Law and Order Team moved up to the Big League, another new member was added, Mr. Charles W. Colson. Mr. Colson learned fast. In the 1970 off-year congressional elections Senator Joseph D. Tydings was defeated in his Maryland reelection bid. One of the major factors in his defeat was a story in *Life* magazine that Tydings used his prestige to land a $7 million Government loan benefiting a firm in which he had acquired a large

'OK. You can come out and take over again.'

financial interest. There were rumors at the time that the White House played a key role in the preparation of the *Life* article. The White House responded by saying, "Any suggestion that the White House would have been involved in the discussion with *Life* regarding the publishing of this story would be incorrect."

However, it was disclosed in 1971 that a member of the White House *had* met several times with the *Life* reporter and, indeed, supplied the pivotal fact upon which *Life* based its story. Unfortunately for Tydings, the White House did not supply the *real* key fact: that the Government investigation cleared Senator Tydings of any irregularity in the processing of the loan. That little trick was turned by the new team member, Mr. Colson.

By then the team had aquired another new member, Attorney General John Mitchell who said, "I am first and foremost a law-enforcement officer." He then proceeded to permit non-enforcement of the Corrupt Practices Act by allowing twenty Nixon-Agnew committees and fifty-two congressmen to violate, without prosecution, its provisions regarding the filing of campaign expenses.

Mitchell, however, did manage to orchestrate the mass arrest of 13,400 U.S. citizens in May of 1971 for the grievous act of assembling to protest the Vietnam war.

Coach Nixon, when asked about the gross suspension of Constitutional rights demonstrated by the mass arrests, replied, "I think when you talk about suspending Constitutional rights, that this is really an exaggeration of what was done." Regarding police tactics, he added, "I approve of what they did, and in the event that we have similar situations in the future, I hope that we can handle those situations as well as this was handled."

What "they did" that Mr. Nixon was so proud of, according to the U.S. Court of Appeals, was illegally arrest approximately 13,200 citizens and caused the District of Columbia government to fork out over $37,000 in damages as a result of a lawsuit.

But then freedom of speech has never been a high priority item with the Law and Order Team. For example, when Pentagon cost ana-

lyst A. Ernest Fitzgerald was battling for reinstatement after he had been fired for speaking out on cost overruns, the team reaction was this note to H. R. Haldeman: "Fitzgerald is no doubt a top-notch cost expert, but he must be given very low marks in loyalty; and after all, loyalty is the name of the game." The note then recommended: "We should let him bleed, for awhile at least. Any rush to pick him up and put him back on the Federal payroll will be tantamount to an admission of earlier wrongdoing on our part."

Occasionally a member of the team would get the signals crossed and strike out in the wrong direction. On March 13, 1971, the Agriculture Department announced that there would be no increase in price supports for the dairy industry. Naturally, the Dairy Lobby didn't think that was a very friendly move and Coach Nixon agreed. So on March 23, the coach had a meeting with dairy representatives to set things straight.

A letter from William A. Powell, president of Mid-America Dairymen, Inc., who attended the meeting, pointed out how friendly Nixon could be: "He (Nixon) said, 'You people are my friends and I appreciate it.' Two days later an order came from the U.S. Department of Agriculture increasing the support price of milk to eighty-five percent of parity, which added from $500 to $700 million to dairy farmers' milk checks. We can't afford to overlook this kind of economic benefit. Whether we like it or not, this is the way the system works."

Of course friendship from a Law and Order Team seeking reelection doesn't come cheap. According to court records, Nixon's personal lawyer, Mr. Herbert Kalmbach, became the major solicitor in collecting a $400,000 payoff from the friendly dairy folks.

Another friendly bunch were those fellows over at ITT. They were always writing memos, some addressed endearingly to "Dear Ted (Agnew)" or "Dear John (Mitchell)." Unfortunately, one of those memos, written by ITT lobbyist Dita Beard tying a $400,000 contribution to efforts to settle an anti-trust suit, ended up in the hands of columnist Jack Anderson who thought it a bit too friendly.

The Law and Order Team, knowing what a strain the disclosure would place on Ms.

'Speaking of cracking down on lawbreakers . . .'

Beard, did the friendly thing and sent G. Gordon Liddy over to take her to a hospital. Mr. Liddy was not too familiar with the Washington area so he took her to the nearest hospital he could find — which happened to be in Denver, Colorado.

All was not sweetness and light in the ITT deal, however. Then Deputy Attorney Richard Kleindienst was preparing to carry an appeal to the Supreme Court in an attempt to establish the principle that business competition can be unlawfully hindered by growth of conglomerates (ITT), which expand by acquiring unrelated businesses.

Loyal team member John Ehrlichman called Kleindienst and said the President was "directing" him not to file any appeal. Kleindienst replied that he could not do that. Ehrlichman said, "Oh? We'll see about that!"

Then, according to *Newsweek*, which was quoting Kleindienst, Nixon called Kleindienst and asked him, "You son of a bitch, don't you understand the English language?" Nixon then ordered him to drop the appeal. Ultimately Kleindienst had to threaten to resign in order to get the directive rescinded.

Evidently time and circumstances healed the breach, because in March of 1972 Mr. Kleindeinst testified under oath that: "In the discharge of my responsibilities as the acting Attorney General in these (ITT) cases, I was not interfered with by anybody at the White House. I was not importuned; I was not pressured; I was not directed."

Of course Nixon has never ranked the Federal courts very high on his loyalty chart, what with their permissive ways. After his election he tried to correct that by attempting to appoint a succession of legal midgets.

He did manage to find a three-judge panel of the Federal District Court loyal enough to briefly abridge freedom of the press for the first time in our history by restraining publication of the so-called Pentagon Papers. Fortunately, the Supreme Court could not stomach prior restraint and held the Constitution in higher esteem than the Government's pride.

By this time the Nixon team was building its reputation as a law and order outfit by introducing such jewels as preventive detention and no-knock laws. The chief law enforcement officer, Mr. Mitchell, came up with the ultimate legal weapon, the inherent right to wiretap anything that moves and talks — without a court order. That the Supreme Court rejected unanimously.

In the Nixon game plan, what was law for some of us was not binding for them. Tom Wicker, incisive *New York Times* columnist, wrote about an administration official who was required to administer a provision in a law passed by Congress that he felt was unenforceable. The official conferred with John Ehrlichman and suggested either immediately trying to change the law, or make an effort to enforce the provision for awhile to demonstrate to Congress the weakness of the law.

Instead of accepting either recommendation, Ehrlichman simply ordered the official to ignore the provision. "But we can't do that. Congress passed it. It's the law!" the official protested. "Do you mean to tell me," Ehrlichman demanded, "that if Congress does something that's not in the public interest, the President does not have the power to set it aside?"

Back in those days, the Nixon team had a nice law and order creed: "Watch what we do, not what we say." In the very near future that advice would be taken, quite literally.

April 28, 1972

THE MILWAUKEE JOURNAL
TM ® All rights reserved
Publishers-Hall Syndicate

'I can't believe you swallowed that WHOLE thing!'

'Gee Whiz! Can I help it if he followed me home?'

THE MILWAUKEE JOURNAL

THE MILWAUKEE JOURNAL
TM ® All rights reserved
Publishers-Hall Syndicate

October 29, 1972

Double Barreled

July 16, 1970

'It's a model for the entire nation.'

THE MILWAUKEE JOURNAL

'Never mind the small print, my dear. Just sign on the dotted line!'

May 19, 1971

THE MILWAUKEE JOURNAL

'Yes, sir, chief. There won't be a more orderly nation in the world
. . . except maybe the Soviet Union.'

'Anyone who has Mitchell for attorney general, Strom Thurmond as an adviser, the D.C. crime bill for a model and Spiro Agnew as vice president could have made the same mistake, sir.'

'Yes, sir, you're my kind of vice-president!'

THE MILWAUKEE JOURNAL
Publishers-Hall Syndicate, 1973

'The job of vice president may not be much, but the ripoff fringe benefits are great!'

October 18, 1973

IT'S DISGRACEFUL THE WAY THE NEWS MEDIA PRINTED ALL THOSE LEAKS ABOUT MR. AGNEW!

FUNNY! I DON'T REMEMBER YOU COMPLAINING WHEN J. EDGAR HOOVER DECLARED THE BERRIGAN BROTHERS GUILTY BEFORE THEY WERE EVEN CHARGED. . . .

...OR BEING UPSET AT WHITE HOUSE LEAKS ON CONSPIRACY CHARGES AGAINST VIETNAM PROTESTERS.

THAT'S DIFFERENT! THOSE VICTIMS WEREN'T EVEN REPUBLICANS!

REALLY?

THE MILWAUKEE JOURNAL
Publishers-Hall Syndicate, 1973

153

'Anybody in the Justice Department showing signs of pain yet?'

August 22, 1973

THE MILWAUKEE JOURNAL
Publishers-Hall Syndicate, 1973

'You men behind me keep an eye out for bushwhackers!'

THE MILWAUKEE JOURNAL
Publishers-Hall Syndicate, 1973

"Gee, I wonder if I could qualify for some of those government fringe benefits?"

'Look on the bright side, coach. We've got
nowhere to go but up!'

April 6, 1972

WHERE DID WE GO WRONG IN THE BERRIGAN CASE?

U.S. JUSTICE DEPT.

FIRST WE GOT J. EDGAR HOOVER TO PRONOUNCE THEM GUILTY OF CONSPIRACY . . .

THEN WE SET OUT TO PROVE IT BY ENTRAPMENT.

SOMETIMES IT SEEMS THERE IS NO JUSTICE!

FORTUNATELY.

THE MILWAUKEE JOURNAL

159

'Boy! It's a relief to hear that!'

'There! Don't you feel much safer already?'

June 6, 1972

THE MILWAUKEE JOURNAL
TM ® All rights reserved
Publishers-Hall Syndicate

'Aw, what're a few conflict of interest stock deals? I was afraid you might be one of those liberals like Fortas.'

'Say Chief. We've let this robe out about as far as we can and it still doesn't fit.'

December 12, 1969

There Go De Judge

'Introducing your next U.S. Supreme Court Justice . . . a legal giant of our time . . . good old Harrold Whats-his-name!'

'We don't believe in forcing a balance in schools . . . only on
the Supreme Court.'

TM ® All rights reserved 1970
Publishers-Hall Syndicate

THE MILWAUKEE JOURNAL

'Scrape the bottom? What do you think we just did?'

May 20, 1970

Have Gun Will Travel

'Here they call it unwarranted and inexcusable. In my
law book it's called second degree murder.'

"*Pilate took water and washed his hands before the multitude, saying, 'I am innocent of the blood of this just person.'*"

'But what will us sportsmen do for a hobby?'

'When I said we must stop all this senseless killing,
I meant in Southeast Asia!'

'Fire! Fire! Fire!'

September 13, 1972

'I brought you something to read while you're
nursing your wounds!'

For his supporting role in "How I learned to stop worrying and love the ABM system."

December 28, 1972

'I don't know what possessed him . . .expressing a critical opinion like that!'

The Honor Code, Updated

September 10, 1972

THE MILWAUKEE JOURNAL
TM ® All rights reserved
Publishers-Hall Syndicate

'Half a block of ice is better than none, I always say!'

June 10, 1973

'Now that I think of it, there may have been some abuse of Phase 3 wage guidelines.'

THE MILWAUKEE JOURNAL

Middleman

July 22, 1973

'Sorry, chief, but we're having to revise our
revised revision!'

'Relax. I just saved you from a figment of our critic's imagination.'

'No kidding.'

Run for the Oval Room

In May 1973, I received a phone call from a woman in Fort Wayne, Indiana. She had just seen a cartoon I drew that was critical of the President's Watergate speech of April 30. She called to tell me what an affront it was to the Office of the Presidency. She added that even if the President had "done some of those things," the press should not criticize him publicly because it damages respect for the office and our image abroad.

That woman's view represents a fairly common doctrine that has evolved in this country regarding the highest office in the land. It is a doctrine which has its roots in our religious-political mythology — that we are somehow a God-chosen nation and our President is the High Priest. That concept carries with it a counter doctrine that has also evolved over the years. That is, the process by which one achieves the highest office in the land is inherently tainted.

This was graphically illustrated in the results of a poll a few years ago. The overwhelming percentage of the respondents said the highest aspirations they could conceive of for their offspring was to become President of the United States. Yet less than thirty-eight percent of those interviewed said they would like their children to get into politics.

This religious-political doctrine is buttressed by a communications illiteracy that has dulled our critical senses and made us largely a nation of non-readers and non-thinkers. Otherwise there is no credible rationale to explain why Watergate was given such a disinterested view during the summer and fall of 1972.

What George McGovern said about Watergate was "just politics." What the newspapers printed was generally discounted, if read at all. Most Americans got their basic news from television, therefore what they learned about Watergate was taken from a thirty-minute evening newscast.

In its tinsel tradition, television gave them an announcer saying, "The *Washington Post* today alleged such-and-such," and then live from the White House a representative of the High Priest would appear to deny the report. What the public got from television was a *dispute*, not a scandal.

The long, winding trail down into credibility canyon started right after the break-in and arrests:

• White House press secretary Ron Ziegler: "I'm not going to comment from the White House on a third-rate burglary attempt . . . . I'm sure certain elements are trying to stretch this into something more than it is."

• Richard Nixon in his first response to the issue: "The White House has no involvement whatever in this particular incident."

'Great! I have a suggestion as to where you can start!'

• Ron Ziegler on the press disclosure of the link between Donald Segretti and White House aide Dwight Chapin: "I will not dignify with comment stories based on hearsay, character assassination, innuendo or guilt by association."

• Ron Ziegler on the press disclosure of a secret campaign fund controlled by White House chief of staff H. R. Haldeman: "Shabby journalism . . . a blatant effort at character assassination . . . ."

• Ron Ziegler, nine days after Mr. Nixon said that he had launched his own investigation: "As we have said before, nobody in the White House had any involvement or prior knowledge of that event. I repeat that statement today."

Finally, when these remarks crumbled under their own weight, the White House calmly told the nation that their past statements were "inoperative," a neat word for lies. Like an episode out of a Saturday afternoon serial, President Nixon struggled to extricate himself from the quicksand of deceit, only to sink deeper into the mire.

One must minutely examine the web of Nixon semantics to catch a glimpse of the truth, for it is as elusive as a spider's trail darting in and out of view among the rays of the morning sun.

For example, there is his handling of the Ellsberg burglary. The President explained: "On May 22, I said that it wasn't until the time of my own investigation that I learned of the break-in at the office of Mr. Ellsberg's psychiatrist and I specifically authorized the furnishing of this information to Judge Byrne. After a very careful review, I have determined that this statement of mine was not precisely accurate. It was on March 17 that I first learned of the break-in at the office of Dr. Fielding, and that was four days before the beginning of my own investigation on March 21."

The elusion was a confession of a seemingly insignificant four-day discrepancy in date. The truth is that for thirty-nine days, Nixon withheld criminal evidence from a trial that was in progress. It was not until April 25 that he agreed to turn over the evidence. Those thirty-nine days were a *prima facia* example of misprison of a felony, which is, itself, a felony.

Then, thirty-nine days after he "learned" of the burglary, Nixon authorized John Ehrlichman to approach Judge Byrne with the possibility of Byrne becoming head of the FBI.

The ultimate convolution came with Nixon's rationale regarding the dialogue over reporting the burglary to Judge Byrne. Nixon said he was advised by Attorney General Kleindeinst that it was not strictly necessary to report the break-in because the burglars were not successful in finding what they wanted. Nixon accepted that piece of legal nonsense by his own admission. A first-year law student would give the President failing grades on all three of the above points.

Then there was the elusion in Nixon's television speech responding to the major charges brought before the Senate Committee: "At first I entrusted the task of getting me the facts to Mr. Dean. When, after spending a week at Camp David, he failed to produce the written report I had asked for, I turned to John Ehrlichman and the attorney general — while also making independent inquiries of my own. By mid-April I had received Mr. Ehrlichman's report and also one from the attorney general based on new information uncovered by the Justice Department. These reports made it clear to me that the situation was far more serious than I had imagined."

It is enlightening to measure that elusion against the unchallenged events of that "mid-April" — April 15 to be exact. On that day, Assistant Attorney General Henry Petersen visited the President and warned him that his chief aides, H. R. Haldeman, John Ehrlichman and John Dean might be criminally prosecuted. Petersen recommended immediate dismissal of Haldeman and Ehrlichman. In his testimony before the Senate Committee, Petersen said the President asked if John Dean, then supplying information to Federal prosecutors, should also be fired, and Petersen said no, "We don't want to give the impression that he is being subjected to reprisal because of his cooperation."

What action did President Nixon take based on "new information uncovered by the Justice

November 27, 1972

'We must end this whole era of permissiveness
. . . present company excepted, of course!'

Department" that was "far more serious" than he had "imagined"? Suspend the three men until further investigation?

Hardly. Within twenty-four hours he was demanding John Dean's resignation, and within three days he had entrusted to H. R. Haldeman material so secret that its existence was unknown to the Justice Department — the White House tapes. One may legitimately ask, Didn't Mr. Nixon believe Mr. Petersen's information regarding Haldeman? If not, why did he refer to the assistant attorney general in that same speech as a Government employee with an "impeccable" record?

After it was subsequently disclosed that Haldeman had reviewed some of the tapes, senior White House aides explained that he did so to check the charges Dean had made against the President. But the fact was that no charges had been made in "mid-April" by Dean.

Then there is a veritable gold mine of lesser illusions.

At President Nixon's October press conference, he alluded to an historical precedent to justify his proposed "tape compromise." He told of how Chief Justice John Marshall had subpoenaed a letter written by Thomas Jefferson during the Aaron Burr treason trial. According to Nixon, Jefferson produced a "summary" of the contents of a letter which was relevant to the trial and that compromise was accepted by Justice Marshall.

The historical reality is that Jefferson *did* comply with the subpoena and submitted the *entire* letter to a U.S. Attorney who then decided what was to be excised and what would be relevant to the trial.

Speaking of the relationship of the tapes compromise to the firing of Special Prosecutor Archibald Cox, Nixon wove another little illusion: "Attorney General Richardson approved this proposition; Senator Baker, Senator Ervin approved this proposition. Mr. Cox was the only one that rejected it."

The reality was that the same "compromise" Richardson, Ervin and Baker approved was not the same compromise offered to Cox. The formula presented to Cox had an added provision that no other Presidential tapes, notes or memoranda were to be sought through the judicial process by the special prosecutor. All three men, Richardson, Ervin and Baker — when they learned of this addendum — supported Cox in his refusal to accept it.

Moreover, there are too many unanswered questions that stretch the President's credibility beyond the brink of tolerance:

• Why, after his personal lawyer, Herbert Kalmbach, testified under oath as to the connection between political saboteur Donald Segretti and White House aide Dwight Chapin, didn't the President summon Kalmbach and question him on that and other possible White House involvement?

• Why, if there were no personal wrongdoing on his part, would the President be so adamant about releasing memoranda regarding the ITT and Dairy Lobby contributions?

• Why would a President, so desperately searching for the truth, fail to question Acting FBI Director L. Patrick Gray at length after he warned Nixon that men around him were trying to "mortally" wound him?

• For that matter, why didn't the President fire Gray on the spot when Gray admitted destroying Watergate evidence? Or at very least question Gray about the incidents surrounding their destruction?

• Why, after the first press reports, did the President authorize the release of misleading figures in regard to money spent on his private homes if there was nothing improper about the expenditures?

• Why, if the White House tapes symbolized the ultimate principle of executive privilege, did the President finally decide to turn them over to Federal District Judge John Sirica rather than appeal to the Supreme Court?

Ultimately, the historical measure of Watergate will not be resolution of the criminal accusations involved — which include illegal wiretapping, perjury, misrepresentation of facts material to an investigation, misprison of a felony, obstruction of justice, bribery and tampering with a witness, and removing, damaging and destroying official records.

June 27, 1973

'1984 came a little early this century.'

(It is useful to detail these terms because of the fog of obfuscations that has rolled over them. Breaking and entering became "intelligence gathering operations," burglars became "plumbers" and Government-perpetrated crimes became "White House horrors." Stefan Kanfer, writing in *Time* magazine, put it beautifully: "Euphemisms are to the tongue, what novocain is to the gums.")

These things will pass into history as mere symptoms of the spreading corruption and unprecedented usurpation and misuse of Government power. The real judgement of history will come to rest on how we, as a nation of free peoples, respond to the cancer we have discovered in our body politic.

We have brought to power a man so petty that he pilfers tax money to enhance his private home. We have brought to power a man so callous that he would wiretap his own brother. We have brought to power a man so isolated from reality and so obsessed with image and power that he was willing to subvert civil liberties and the democratic process to maintain them. We have brought to power a man who installed the most dangerously corrupt administration in the history of this country.

It was not a corruption of thievery and graft, as was the case with the administrations of Harding and Grant. Rather, it was corruption by an administration of hypocrites. These were the zealous champions of law and order. These were self-righteous men who anointed themselves as keepers of the national morals.

In the end they corrupted the instruments of power for the single purpose of maintaining power. In doing so, they attempted to steal our birthright — a citizen's privilege to choose his President in a reasonably democratic fashion. It is the type of corruption that has always been a signpost to dictatorship.

We should not be diverted by the admonition not to wallow in Watergate — that there is more pressing and important business such as the Middle East and détente.

This is, on its face, a specious argument. What claim can we place on world moral leadership when we are morally bankrupt at the White House? How can we be a force for freedom abroad when the very instruments of our democracy are coated with the rust of corruption? The *true* root of our security is the value of our free institutions.

This nation should demand the impeachment of Richard Nixon.

To do less is a vote of no confidence in our system of government. To do less is to confess that the institutions of this great nation are so fragile that only one man can control our destiny. To do less is to forever codify the principle that once a man is elected to the Presidency, he becomes the sole interpreter of the law and may choose to place himself above it without recourse.

If we accept that principle, we will not have simply reached the end of Watergate — we will have reached the end as a democratic society.

THE MILWAUKEE JOURNAL
Publishers-Hall Syndicate, 1973

'Maybe we could get 'em to build _us_ a beach cabana, storage
shed, redwood fence and put in electric heating, too. We got
as many kooks and Commies here as they have out
in San Clemente.'

F. DONALD NIXON

THE MILWAUKEE JOURNAL
Publishers-Hall Syndicate, 1973

Big Brother

'No, dear, they weren't on trial . . . they were the prosecuting team.'

July 12, 1973

THE MILWAUKEE JOURNAL

'Now let's go over that part again, Alice, where
you slipped and fell into the rabbit hole.'

'Well, I just hope you don't get one of those
awful criminal-coddling judges, John.'

April 18, 1973

THE MILWAUKEE JOURNAL
Publishers-Hall Syndicate, 1973

'I have just discovered major new developments
in the Watergate case.'

'. . . moving along to the important issues . . . Europe, the Middle East . . .'

July 9, 1973

Dear Senator Ervin:—
   Your request for the documents of my top aides relating to Watergate has come to my attention.
   No president accused of covering up burglary, illegal

wiretapping, hush-money pay-offs, crooked campaign funds and generally subverting the democratic process, could function if his aides' papers were open to public scrutiny!

Therefore, in the name of national Security, the Constitution, and Mother's Day, I must decline.
   Yours truly,
   Richard M. Nixon

P.S. Trust me!

SANDERS

THE MILWAUKEE JOURNAL
Publishers-Hall Syndicate, 1973

July 27, 1973

THE MILWAUKEE JOURNAL   Publishers-Hall Syndicate, 1973

'Ah'm jes a lil' ol' country lawyer, Mr. Goliath, but lemme
show you this here trick ah larned . . .'

October 31, 1972

THE MILWAUKEE JOURNAL
Publishers-Hall Syndicate, 1973

'I don't care if high government officials corrupted the courts, FBI, CIA, Justice Department and the democratic process! I want to see I Love Lucy!'

September 22, 1972

THE MILWAUKEE JOURNAL

THE MILWAUKEE JOURNAL
Publishers-Hall Syndicate, 1973

March 5, 1973

THE MILWAUKEE JOURNAL   Publishers-Hall Syndicate, 1973

August 20, 1973

Publishers-Hall Syndicate, 1973   THE MILWAUKEE JOURNAL

"Well, well. If it isn't the man in charge of the 'most intensive' investigation 'ever conducted'."

September 19, 1972

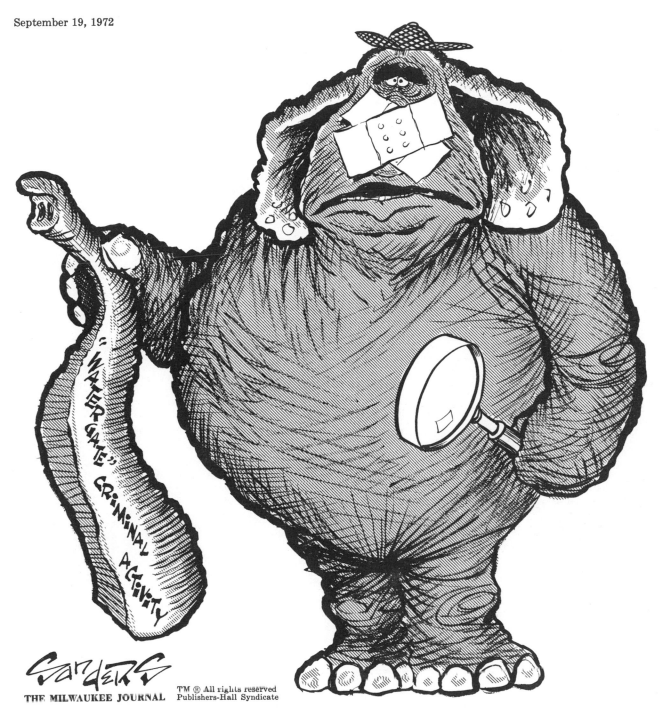

'After an exhaustive investigation I find this elephant trunk, acting independently and of its own accord, guilty of. . . .'

THE MILWAUKEE JOURNAL
Publishers-Hall Syndicate, 1973

June 7, 1973

'If the president is involved, I don't want to know about it.'
—Mel Laird

THE MILWAUKEE JOURNAL   Publishers-Hall Syndicate, 1973

". . . and once more the spheroid flew, but Casey still ignored it, and the umpire said, 'Strike two!'"

October 21, 1973

THE MILWAUKEE JOURNAL
Publishers-Hall Syndicate, 1973

THE MILWAUKEE JOURNAL
Publishers-Hall Syndicate, 1973

October 22, 1973

Sanders

THE MILWAUKEE JOURNAL
Publishers-Hall Syndicate, 1973

'Sure I did it. What are you going to do about it?'

'And should you have any problems, just come to me. I'm sure we can work something out.'

October 25, 1973

'Quick! Toss out the tapes! Maybe that will slow 'em down!'

Identified Flying Object

November 2, 1973

THE MILWAUKEE JOURNAL
Publishers-Hall Syndicate, 1973

Rose Mary's Baby

January 17, 1974

'How about this? While Rose Mary Woods answered the phone,
a mouse accidentally ran back and forth across the tape
recorder keyboard five to nine times.'

THE MILWAUKEE JOURNAL
Publishers-Hall Syndicate, 1974

'It's the FBI, sir. They'd like to question you about a
Uher 5000 tape recorder.'

January 29, 1974

THE MILWAUKEE JOURNAL
Publishers-Hall Syndicate, 1974